The Ultimate Ortho Handbook
Seven Essential Success Strategies
They Never Taught You in Dental School

Dustin S. Burleson, DDS

Adjunct Assistant Professor, Department of Orthodontics, UMKC School of Dentistry

Attending Orthodontist, The Children's Mercy Hospital, Kansas City, MO

Director, Rheam Foundation for Cleft and Craniofacial Orthodontics

Founder and President, Burleson Orthodontics & Pediatric Dentistry

Founder and Senior Consultant, Burleson Seminars

Voted Best Dad in the World by Two-Thirds of His Children

The Ultimate Ortho Handbook

Seven Essential Success Strategies They Never Taught You In Dental School

Copyright © 2014 by Burleson Media Group

ISBN (978-0-9913468-0-6)

Dedication

To the hopes and dreams that burned inside of every doctor when they applied to professional school. May your goodwill and love for the profession continue to inspire the next generation of doctors.

To Sam, Will and Ben for inspiring me to work hard, serve others, and smile. I love you.

Table of Contents

Preface

The Orthodontic Model Needs to be Completely Reinvented

They must often change, who would be constant in happiness or wisdom.

– CONFUCIUS

Politically-correct and wimpy orthodontists, take caution. This book is not for those who wish to be liked nor those who like to make excuses. No, the strategies presented here are for a very specific type of doctor. The doctor who wishes to be respected but successful beyond his wildest imagination. The doctor who dreams of enhancing the impact on his family, employees, patients, profession and community. These are the heroes of this handbook.

You might have found this book from a friend, colleague or because you were searching for new and exciting ways to invigorate your practice. Perhaps you've noticed more competition in your area and you've heard of me and my success with transforming the practices of hundreds of doctors all over the globe (seven countries as of this writing) who wish to break free from the chains of private practice.

If you know me and my track record, then you've probably been motivated to study my practices and newsletters to discover how to build the practice of your dreams, on your terms and ethically grow a patient-centered practice with wild success. You understand that I'm an average Joe from Kansas City. I am not exceptionally charismatic. I do not possess any super-human strengths or special gifts. I'm just a disciplined guy who pays attention and has figured out a few things on my journey to build one of the fastest-growing orthodontic practices in North America. Our growth post-recession has been 638 percent. I work one day per week in the clinic. I spend the rest of my time sailing with my family or volunteering my time with the cleft palate foundation I started and donating more free cases to Smiles Change Lives than any other doctor in the country.

It didn't start out this way. I've been poor. I've had the money run out (way) before the end of the month. I've worked 90 hour weeks and pulled 37 all-nighters in my first year of opening a from-scratch practice. I've stared bankruptcy in the face and I've had my entire staff walk out on me one cold day in February 2009. Short version of that story: I deserved it. I'm the furthest thing from perfect you can find on the planet. I've also had the exceptional fortune to grow up in a family with 12 dentists and make every mistake in the book early in my career. Before the age of twenty-six I had already owned three businesses. When my friends were going to the lake in their twenties, I was filing trademark and copyright applications and defending myself in a few lawsuits of my own. I've stirred the pot. I've been bitten in the ass. I've had the dental board call my office after complaints from my competitors and sent or received more cease and desist letters in the last year than you've likely received wedding invitations in your entire life. From the scars and battle wounds, I've emerged victorious with only the systems and strategies that work. Period.

The systems and strategies we share with coaching clients all over the globe, who are on a waiting list to give me checks as high as $35,000 per year, are tried and true. They are a shortcut to the future you've dreamed of in orthodontics. The same future you envisioned when you applied to residency. Unfortunately, becoming a doctor and orthodontic specialist entitles you to nothing. Get over it.

If you realize the orthodontic model needs to be blown up and completely reinvented, this book is for you. If you think what got you here will get you through the next ten or twenty years, you are in for a shocking surprise. Competition, Invisalign, Six-Month Smiles and "instant orthodontics" (i.e. veneers) have dropped a bomb on the orthodontic world we enjoyed a few short decades ago. Whining and complaining about it won't help you an iota. Getting serious about your future will. Better to seek out mentors to shine the light on the mistakes they've made and the best practices that are killing it in their practices. And that's exactly the aim of this book.

If you will seriously implement the seven strategies presented here, your practice will soar and your personal freedom and liberation from the wear and tear of running a practice will finally set you free to serve others with passion, make more money, give generously to your employees and community and create an amazing legacy in the process.

Don't envy those of us enjoying a liberated practice lifestyle with complete personal and financial freedom. Join us.

– Dustin S. Burleson, DDS

Introduction

Set Goals, Take Action & Repeat

Do you want to know who you are? Don't ask. Act!
Action will delineate and define you.

– THOMAS JEFFERSON

This is no ordinary practice management book for the average orthodontist doing just one job. This book is specifically for the doctor who wears many hats and understands that treating patients is the easiest part of his day. This book will help drastically re-engineer all of the things they never taught you in dental school but that you have likely been doing wrong for years. If the strategies in this book are applied faithfully, your practice will soar and your personal freedom and liberation from the wear and tear of running a practice will finally set you free to serve others with passion, make more money, give generously to your employees and community and create an amazing legacy in the process.

This book will challenge you to confront the strategies presented with an open mind. Take notes, implement each concept into your practice and transform your personal and professional productivity.

You will discover how to:

Stop wasting your money on marketing that doesn't work. Keep your patients and referring dentists engaged every month and transform them into "raving fans" of your office. Beware the practice consultant who tells you all of your problems will be solved if you just double the number of new patients in your practice. Without the correct internal systems in place, you are flushing your marketing investments of time and money straight down the drain. If you insist on following advice that doubles or triples the number of non-ideal new patients in your practice without first implementing proven internal systems and second realizing everyone with a pulse is not your ideal patient, please save your money and mail it to my cleft palate foundation so at least *someone* can benefit from your folly.

Discover the biggest mistake I made in building my practice and how to avoid it. Run from this costly pitfall and watch your practice soar. How you address this issue in your practice will, hands down, determine your success and to a large extent, your bank account. Doctors who retire with epic retirements and live life on their own terms all got this right in their practices. Stop the inevitable insanity that results from ignoring this.

Steal my perfect formula for compelling content that attracts patients to you like moths to a flame. Your patients don't want to be bored. They want to be wowed. Most doctors ignore this advice, to their peril. When I spend the first day in private coaching with new clients, I can tell within 3-4 minutes if they are approaching this issue correctly or not. Fixing the problem is simple and creates a multiple net seven-figure swing in their practices over a career. If I had told them they could fly to Kansas City and make a million dollars or more over the lifetime of their practice within the first 3-4 minutes, they would have told me "impossible." The truth – it is possible and we do it every day for our clients who implement and take action towards a better, bigger and brighter future for themselves.

DID YOU KNOW...

15%

of Orthodontists invest more than $1,500 per year marketing their practices. 15% of Orthodontists are extremely optimistic about their future. Coincidence?

Is your practice heading in the right direction?

Focus on the five things to avoid in your practice marketing. Get this right and your return on investment will skyrocket. Hint: your competitors are doing this entirely wrong. The average orthodontist spent less than $1,500 marketing his practice last year. Sadly, even that small investment was probably wasted. You will not get rich by blindly copying the marketing and advertising strategies of big dumb companies. I hate to be the bearer of bad news, but you do not have a $100 million marketing budget. You cannot afford to waste a penny on marketing this year, next year, ever.

Appreciate the only metric you should be worried about in today's economy and slow-to-no growth professions of dentistry and orthodontics. This is the ticket to extreme success. When you discover how simple the concept is to implement, you might cry tears of joy and frustration. Joy for the newfound productivity and frustration for all of the years you *coul* *have* been reaping the rewards of this strategy. And so it goes with each strategy and concept presented here. The average orthodontist will say "that would *never* work for me." The smartest doctors in the room will ask "how *can* this work for me?" Your job is to turn over every stone. Look for the ways these strategies can work for you. Discard the baggage you've been carrying with you for ten, twenty or even thirty years. Yes, the profession of orthodontics needs to be completely reinvented. Now is the time.

Let's get started.

Chapter One

It's Not About You

Service to others is the rent you pay for your room here on earth.

– MUHAMMAD ALI

If you find yourself staring at the title to this chapter and thinking I'm nuts I will tell you again that I've been where you are. So I know what you are thinking. I know that when you graduated dental school and officially became a doctor that you thought it all became about you, your position of authority and near-certain guarantee of success and prosperity. I'm here to tell you loud and clear that it's not.

It really is not about you, doctor.

It is about so much more than *you* and your white coat. And if you only focus on yourself, extreme success will never be yours. Never. Remove the focus from yourself and your power as the doctor in your practice, as difficult as that may be, and focus instead on the areas that matter. I promise you that when you do, great things are going to happen. Learn to step aside and shine the spotlight on the areas of your practice that can produce insane results. Hear me out on this one…

When I say that it's *not* about you but rather *everything* and *everyone else*, I mean it. Starting with your staff. When you develop a rock star staff and trust them with the responsibility to serve your patients with excellence, you take consistent steps in building a business that doesn't hinge on your every word, every decision, every action. How much attention have you placed in hiring the proper staff? The team you have working with you will make a world of difference in your overall success. You simply can't be all things to all people and in all places at once. During my diagnostic and prescriptive phone consultations with new clients who have paid me upwards of $35,000 to fix their practices, I can determine within three or four minutes whether I'm dealing with a practice where *nothing* happens without the doctor's approval, versus a real business with real assets and income you can only imagine.

Your office needs to run like a well-oiled machine. Today's health care practices are *too complex* to assume that you can do everything. You simply can't do it all; and if you try, your results will be minuscule compared to your true potential. You must have the right people performing the right job in every position. Each employee must have the tools they need to effectively do their jobs and they must be on the same page with your company goals and office protocols. Most importantly, you have given them the permission and responsibility to act and produce results without your interference. Reread that last sentence. This is how you transform your quarterly income into your monthly income. Your annual income into your monthly income. You can't do it on your own. Rockefeller once said "I would rather earn one percent of the efforts from one hundred men than one hundred percent of my own efforts." He knew the secret in leveraging your most-expensive business expense – payroll. Treat your team like gold and they will rise to your expectations almost without fail.

When you have your staff on board with the idea of serving the patient, growing the practice and getting results, you will see that they go above and beyond for you, your patients and your practice. Projects will get completed, operations will run smoothly, and your happy patients will spread the good word about you and your practice time and again. And they can do it without making *you* the primary focus. This all comes down to the idea of treating every patient with an amazing attitude and experience and empowering your employees to be the ones that deliver that experience. Train your employees well and then get out of the way.

Patients come to you because they are seeking something. They want to avoid pain, improve function or achieve a beautiful smile. Who doesn't, right? But many people are fearful and apprehensive about going to the dentist. Even if you help your patient achieve their goals (and more), if your staff doesn't make them feel comfortable, welcomed and special, they will leave your office unsatisfied. Unfortunately, most of the new coaching clients I meet are stuck in the mindset that the doctor has to make every decision, micromanage every task, shoulder the entire responsibility to grow the practice. Most doctors fail to empower their employees and, therefore, fail to deliver exceptional service. You can't do it all. Stop trying. It's actually hurting your results.

This simple strategy has huge implications on your legacy as a doctor and leader in your community. Your legacy is what you will leave behind when you are gone. Think about Walt Disney, Bill Gates, or Steve Jobs. Each of them has a legacy that they are in the midst of creating or have already left behind and each one involved empowering those around them to become better than they ever imagined. Think about that for a minute. Are you instilling more confidence and making a bigger impact in the lives of your employees than even *they* can imagine? The best leaders do.

The Doctor as Practice Leader & Visionary

Your Team of Employees

Your Patients and the Relationship with the List

How will you maximize your impact?

Walt Disney has left behind a legacy that demonstrated what imagination, creativity, and perseverance can do. Disney is one of the worlds most-valuable brands, according to Forbes, employing over 166,000 people and having annual sales more than $40 billion. It's not just about the money, it's about what he started and the legacy he left behind for future generations. Beyond just the money, his legacy touches millions of people each year, and employs more than most companies could ever conceive.

Bill Gates and Steve Jobs already have and are in the process of leaving amazing legacies. But don't feel like you have to generate billions each year in order to for your legacy to matter. That's not the point.

Think about the legacy *you* want to leave behind. Then do things that matter. We go through our lives often times putting too much attention and energy into micromanaging things that don't matter or that are not going to help us build the legacy we want to leave behind. Micromanaging *how* your team gets results and losing sleep because they don't do things exactly the way you would, while failing entirely to measure the *right* statistics in your practice, is absolute insanity. It's time to change that. Think about the legacy you want to leave behind and then take steps to help make that happen. The more you let go of control, the greater your results. Each time I try to gain more control over how my team achieves results, I notice that my results diminish. Learn to let go. Train, delegate responsibility, measure accurately, celebrate or tweak for improvement but do not micromanage. It is the habit of a poor orthodontist.

In order to leave the professional legacy you want you need to think about bigger issues. These include things like:

- Your position in the market.
- How you attract your patients.
- What you say to people and how you say it.
- The degree to which your system could run on autopilot without you there watching over everything.

The last point is especially important for you to be successful in your practice and achieve the level of success you deserve. Recently, on a whim, one of my entrepreneur friends asked me to go to the World Series with him in the middle of the week. Many professionals in my position would not be able to do it because they are afraid their office will be at a stand still or fall apart in their absence. Not me. I went to the game and enjoyed myself. Meanwhile, my offices were still open and running smoothly.

Could you do the same? Does your system support that type of freedom and autonomy? If not, it's time to make some serious changes.

I know how important this issue is because I learned about it the hard way. I didn't always have the great team I have today or the office that runs like a well oiled machine. In fact, this all hit me like a ton of bricks the day my staff walked out on me.

Yes, it was in our early days and we only had three employees but they still walked out on me; teaching me a lesson that nothing else could have. The day your staff walks out on you is the day you will without a doubt learn that it is not all about you. It really isn't.

The sooner you realize that and take action to make it about everyone else, the sooner you will be on your way to a higher level of success. And when you make your staff a high priority you will see how it comes back to you. They will bend over backwards to help you reach your company goals. I can't imagine going back to the days when I thought being a doctor was all bout "being the doctor." The smartest doctors on the planet have realized they must lead a happy team, support their employees with opportunities for growth and responsibility within the practice, and then reap countless rewards. It doesn't work in reverse. You cannot wait for the day when you have massive wealth and *then* start treating your employees like they are gold. You'll never achieve massive wealth this way. Listen, your employees cannot and will not treat your patients they like *they* are number one unless you start treating your employees like *they* are number one.

After interviewing hundreds of employees for our own practices and our coaching clients, training dozens of orthodontic and pediatric dental residents, hiring doctors in my own practices and for my coaching clients, and building extensive training systems to foster growth and success in human capital, I can confidently say that your most-important investment with the largest potential for leverage into wild success is your investment in human capital. Build a team of rock stars that can care for your patients without being micromanaged, train them, encourage them, reward them and then get the hell out of the way. Maintain your position as the visionary leader and cheerleader of your employees, but get out of their way and let them fly. The most-successful doctors in my coaching groups with the highest incomes, the most free time with their families, and in the beginning stages of legacy-building all get this right – they make time in their schedules to put human capital as a top priority.

When was the last time you met with your team to paint the vision in their minds of where your practice will be in three to five years? How often do you encourage your employees to reach higher and grow deeper than even *they* thought possible? Isn't it time you got started?

Chapter Two

If You Build It, They Might Come

*Try, try, try, and keep on trying is the rule that must be followed
to become an expert in anything*

– W. CLEMENT STONE

Quite the contrary, in fact. They probably won't come unless you give them a reason. Just ask the many businesses that close their doors each year whether or not just building it brought people through the door. No, building it is just the beginning.

According to the Small Business Administration about half of all businesses survive to reach the five-year mark. A third of all businesses reach their 10 year anniversary. Statistics aside, one look around your town and you will see first-hand how many businesses don't survive. You can probably rattle off a handful of places that have closed in the last year or two right off the top of your head. We all can. And it's not that these places were horrible. They didn't lack a good idea in what their product or service was. Their owners were likely just as passionate about their business as you are about your practice.

The problem is they probably thought if they built it that people would come. They also probably got into business for the wrong reason. If you ask most small business owners why they started their business, they will state something along the lines of "I was sick and tired of working for someone else." So, they got into business to be their own boss, only to

realize they don't have one boss as a small business owner, they have hundreds of "bosses" (i.e., customers) that hold them accountable every day. They also quickly realize they can't take vacation without the entire operation shutting down. In essence, what they have is a job they can't quit. Couple this with the fact that most small business owners do little or no research into the marketplace to dissuade them from the fact that there are nine other businesses in the same category on the same street also doing poorly. But, darn it, "I'm sick of having a boss and I want to open my own restaurant." This is a very naive way to go into business. But it's not too far from the way most orthodontists go into business. The difference is that we need a license to open our businesses and we also spent ten or eleven years in school preparing to open the darn thing. The odds were in our favor simply based on statistics. Then 2008 happened.

Just like most small business owners, we were immensely spoiled before the recession of 2008. The American consumer had a free-flowing credit line, called a home-equity line of credit. We over spent, under saved, dined out too often and rarely thought about most purchases because our home values continued to increase each year. Until they didn't. Now things are different. Instead of bemoaning the business failures around us, why not learn from them?

Another falsehood in business — do good work and everything else will take care of itself. Not likely. You may be really good at what you do, but being good is just one piece of a complex puzzle. You have to do more than just be good at what you do. You must be *so* good that the right people take notice and are willing to swim through lakes filled with hungry alligators just to get to your front door and wait in line to pay you in full.

To reach the right people, you must consider your market position. If you don't know who you are, what you stand for and who your ideal customer, client or patient is, you will quickly kill your practice or yourself trying to make everyone happy, including the patients that are impossible to please under any circumstance, even if God himself treated the case. Clearly define your position in the market, then go *ominate* it. Articulate who you are for and then go find those patients. Magnetize them to you.

Apple has clearly defined their position in the market. They are for a very specific someone. They are also *not* for a very specific someone. What would happen if Apple tried to be everything to everyone? What if they changed their products to look more like Windows? Would they piss off the die-hard Mac fans? Yes. Would they appease the Windows fans? Not likely. When you try to be everything to everyone, you become nothing to no one. Only after you determine *your* precise position in the market, can you start to build your brand and attract the right customers, clients, patients.

Think about the Ritz Carlton. They too have clearly defined their position in the market. What would happen if the Ritz Carlton resorts tried to appease the same customers looking for a quick, cheap motel on the side of a highway during a long road trip? Vice versa, what if the Motel 8 started acting like the Ritz? Get this clear in your head – neither position in the market is right or wrong, but each position is *exactly* right for each respective business. They are both true to their positions in the market. They know exactly who their specific "someone" is and how to serve him. They make every decision in their business based on their position in the market and staying true to serving their segment appropriately.

Now think about most orthodontic practices? Who do they think their ideal patient is? Everyone. Nearly all of my new coaching clients, on their initial diagnostic phone consultation, believe their market segment includes anyone with teeth. Phooey. I could look at your income statement from last year and quickly tell you who your market segment *shoul* be. Hint: it's usually the top five to twenty percent of your patients who have paid you the overwhelming-majority of your income. If you're not familiar with the 80/20 principle, now would be a good time to look it up. It rings true in nearly every area of your business.

Twenty percent of your patients (sometimes as little as 5 percent) are responsible for eighty percent of your income. What about the bottom of your pyramid? You guessed it. They are they ones who owe you (a lot of) money, won't do anything that insurance doesn't pay for, constantly complain, write negative reviews about your practice on-line, etc. Your best market segment is the top twenty percent of your practice that loves coming to see you, always have fun when they are in the office, refer friends and family, pay without resistance and generally *love* to do business with you. If you can't determine within that segment the precise details that make this group "tick" or if you are new and do not have enough patients, then you can reverse-engineer your market segment instead.

To reverse-engineer your market segment, first determine what sets you apart. What is unique about your practice? In which areas do you frequently receive compliments? Let's say you live in an area that has half a dozen orthodontists that people can choose from. Some areas have many more than that. You must know what sets your practice apart in order to sell your services over your competition. In other words, why would I, a prospective patient of yours presented with all of the choices in the market (including the option of doing nothing) choose to bring my child to your practice?

Claiming your segment of the market and creating effective branding for your business relies upon the fact that you know what sets you apart, why people should choose you over the competition, and so on. Without taking this step so you effectively position yourself, you will not get far in business. Your practice will look like every other office in town and you will likely resort to competing based on price. I've experienced this position firsthand and strongly recommend you avoid it at all costs. Instead, find out what makes you different, share it with the world and price it accordingly. If you need help getting your mind right about your pricing strategy, I strongly urge you to visit a Disney theme park, stay at a Ritz Carlton or Four Seasons, lookup the Kodak study from the 1980s on pricing strategy and devour the book *No B.S. Price Strategy* by Dan Kennedy.

I don't care how good you are, if you don't learn how to market your skills or hire someone who can, you'll never get a chance to share those skills with the world. Too many businesses fail simply because they don't know how to effectively market their product or service. It's just that simple. They advertise their business name, location, phone number, address and hours of operation. From today forward, you will avoid marketing and advertising that includes *only* these five items as your main message. It is a complete waste of your time to behave like other small businesses that don't have a clue how to market or advertise effectively. Your marketing dollars will be held accountable to produce a return on investment. This is not a recreational activity. You do not send marketing dollars out into the world simply to tell people who you are, where you're located and when your office is open. Instead you will educate your prospective patients how your practice is different and how you can help solve their problems better than any other practice in town.

I am not suggesting that you need to be a marketing guru here. But all great leaders know when and where to get the assistance they need. If you don't understand marketing and market positioning, or don't want to dig deeper to learn it, then you must hire someone qualified and experienced to pull it off for you.

There are great doctors all over the country who are in poor locations, don't have a good team working with them, and have no system in place for effectively running day-today operations. What does this amount to? A lot of practices closing down. What's more, there have seen 15 million fewer dental visits each year since the recession hit. The American Dental Association predicts it will be this way for another ten to fifteen more years, at least. Most orthodontic offices across the country have experienced twenty or forty percent decreases in patient volume since 2007. Net income for orthodontists has taken a similar hit. We could possibly be entering a new normal with decreased dental expenditures per capita and you might be left behind if you think what got you here is going to get you through the next ten or twenty years.

Bottom line — you must effectively position your practice if you want to survive. Mandatory classic reading for all of my coaching clients (and all orthodontists who want to retire with money in the bank) includes the book *Positioning: The Battle for Your Mind* by Al Ries and Jack Trout. Particularly Trout's strategy on positioning and differentiation in the market requires your careful study. You must review the classic business literature as diligently as you studied anatomy and occlusion, pathology slides or biomechanics and treatment planning. How you approach business concepts and strategies will determine your success moving forward.

The days when you could graduate from dental school, hang a shingle on your building, put your name on a business card and sit back and wait for new patients to roll through your front door are over. Those days are never coming back. Just because you built an office doesn't mean any patients are coming. Fewer patients with more options including large corporate dental chains, federal health clinics, everyone and their brother doing braces, and mass confusion in the marketplace about what sets *anyone* apart have all contributed to a brave new world in dentistry. Welcome to the wonderful world of business.

Isn't it time you started taking it seriously?

Chapter Three

Everyone is in Sales. Get Over It.

"You don't close a sale; you open a relationship
if you want to build a long-term, successful enterprise."

– PATRICIA FRIPP

That's the truth.

If you want to settle for average and allow half of your efforts to be squandered and walk right out the door, go ahead and be my guest. I'd be happy to start your no-sale appointments in my offices. But since you are reading this and looking for information on being more successful, I don't think that's what you want.   Instead, I want you to imagine the day where your practice starts eighty-five to ninety percent of the new patients who visit your office for complimentary consultations. Can you see your life achieving maximum impact and true wealth, as the owner of a business with desirable assets?   Can you see yourself taking action towards this vision? It all starts with the most-valuable asset in your practice.

The most-valuable asset in your practice is not your building. It is not your equipment, your staff, or your contracts receivable. Not at all. It's certainly not your "hands" as a resident once told me after acquiring significant student loans to become an orthodontist with "magical hands." No, your most valuable asset is your patient list. Specifically, your most-prized asset is the relationship you have built with your list.

Can you list at least ten things you did last month to intentionally strengthen the relationship you have with your patient list? Ah, you haven't put in much effort to build a relationship with them, you say? That's problematic. You have to start making this a priority if you want to have a successful practice. Think about Disney again. People at Disney theme parks don't sit around talking about the mechanics of each ride or the specific features of the seats, hotel beds or wax poetic about the breakfast buffet. Instead they share lengthy stories about their *experiences* with Disney and how their relationship with the characters from a young age and the magic of Disney have kept them coming back over the years. Your practice is no different. Your patients will not sit in the waiting room telling wondrous stories about your bonding agent or your newest flavor of fluoride. They will, however, *rave* about the experience and relationship you have with them if you get this right.

If you have attended any my by-invitation-only sold-out seminars, or if you have seen me on stage in front of thousands of entrepreneurs, you have heard me say that you could take my buildings and burn them to the ground, take my staff and ship them all away to another planet, take my equipment and throw it in the river and just give me six months and my patient list, and I would have it all back. That's the truth. That's because I understand that the most valuable asset I have is the relationship with my patient list. Everything else can be replaced, believe it or not. But the relationship with the patient list is like gold. Better than gold, and it needs to be treated as such and protected.

What are you doing *this month* to build the relationship with your patients? If you don't know the answer, you have room for improvement. Address the issue now, before it is too late. Create a plan, set some goals, and turn your focus to building the relationship with your patients. If you don't take the time to improve the relationship with your patients they might leave in search for someone who will. And there's a good chance one of my clients who gets this right, is already in your area, waiting patiently.

Did you realize that the average orthodontist, or at least 85 percent of them, spends around $1,500 per year promoting and marketing their practices? Think about that for a moment. That's a drop in the bucket. That's not a big enough budget to actually make an effective impact. It's certainly not one that is going to help you gain much market share or create a consistent message for the relationship with your list.

When polled, research shows that around 15 percent of orthodontists feel extremely positive about their future. Only 15 percent. That, unfortunately, does not surprise me one bit. Who are the 15 percent who actually are feeling optimistic? They are the same orthodontists who spend more than $1,500 per year promoting their practices. They get the relationship right and they have realized, very clearly, why they are in business, who they are in business to serve and how to leverage the relationship they have built with the patient list.

The 15 percent who are optimistic are the ones who are specifically investing in new patient acquisition, nurturing their patient relationships, following up with those who are "on the fence" and building systems for staff to create unique, memorable experiences for their patients. Those are the doctors optimistic about their futures. And they should be.

Where do you fall in this category? Isn't it time to stop making the same mistake over and over again? Get off the never-ending bus ride to nowhere and make things happen. It's time to get serious and take effective action toward solutions that will make your practice stand out and become more successful.

Until you get serious about making a change in *this area*, you will not see significant changes taking place in your practice. The reason you are reading this report in the first place is because you want change. You want growth. But you must take action here in order to make things happen.

The action items you need to nail down are relationship building, marketing and staff training so that you can create an experience for your patients unlike any other. As mentioned before, it's okay if you don't understand these strategies like a pro. That is something that you and every one in your practice can learn. It's just a matter of which taking initiative and getting started. Buying this handbook was a good place to start. You are already in the elite category of the top 10 percent of orthodontists who "get it" and understand the future of our profession needs to be completely retooled in order to achieve our personal and financial goals while still maintaining high-quality treatment.

I'm continually shocked at the lack of action our profession has taken in our communication skills, marketing, business management and treatment plan presentations. Patients come to us with a fear of the dentist, a fear of expensive treatment and all of the other unknowns of painful metal braces. Unfortunately, few orthodontists have studied these disciplines seriously and even fewer have a daily, weekly, monthly and quarterly game plan that translates into results.

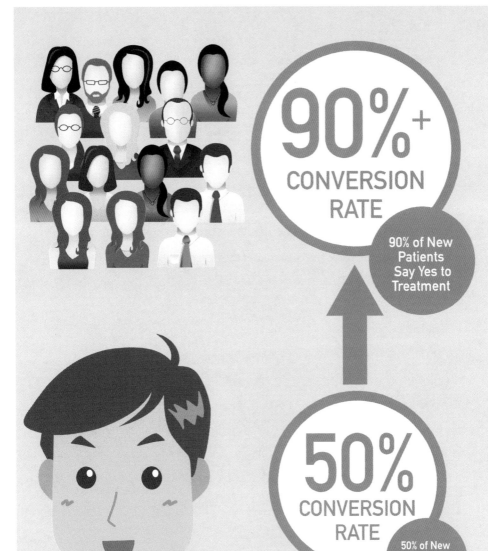

90%+
CONVERSION RATE

90% of New Patients Say Yes to Treatment

50%
CONVERSION RATE

50% of New Patients Say Yes to Treatment

Why not double your practice the smart way?

Our sold-out boot camps consistently take treatment coordinators from the national average of 50-55 percent conversion to consistently above 85 percent (with many doctors above 90 percent). The skills we share are not magical. They do not require that you be exceptionally charismatic. You don't have to "sell" anything. You must only build trust, always act in the patient's best interest, present a solution that is best for each individual patient, and demonstrate confidence as the trusted authority and advisor for the patient or their parent. That's it. It takes only five to seven minutes and can easily convert 85 to 90 percent of your initial consultations into newly-started orthodontic patients.

Unfortunately, most doctors play the game of talking too much, giving too much technical detail about treatment and then walking out of the room and praying that the treatment coordinator closes the case. This is the wrong way to run your practice. If you think you're not guilty of these errors, I challenge you to record your treatment presentations for one week, review them with your treatment coordinator and call me if you think you're doing this one-hundred percent correctly. Hint: if you didn't close 90 percent or more of your cases last week, you've got room for improvement.

The most successful service businesses in the world (think Ritz Carlton, Disney, Nordstrom and the Four Seasons) video tape and secret shop their locations constantly. When was the last time you sent a secret shopper into your practice? Would you want to see the results or would you be hiding under the desk in fear of what you might discover? In our private coaching program, doctors from all over the world are committing to secret shopping their businesses at least quarterly. I've been doing this for years at our practice locations and each time I learn something new.

How long do your new patients wait in the reception area? How does it feel to be a new patient in your practice? How are you greeted? What does the office look like from the patient's perspective? How does it sound, feel and smell in your reception area? Think this is going overboard? Explore the Disney Institute or Ritz Carlton Customer Service training and see what ultimate customer service really looks like.

We all have room for improvement and your practice transformation begins with an honest assessment of the realities in your business. If you can't tell me with near-certainty how much money you will make tomorrow, next week or next month, I can tell you with near-certainty that you're getting this wrong. If you disagree or if you are simply in denial, I encourage you to schedule a secret mystery shopper to visit your practice as a new patient and attend customer service training with Disney or the Ritz Carlton and send me your results. I take this more-seriously than 99 percent of orthodontists and I still learn new things, sometimes painfully, when I have our practices visited by a secret shopper. Without honest assessment, we simply do not know what is going on in our practices. I encourage at-least quarterly assessment but, more-effectively, each month.

Resources

Mystery Shopping Providers Association
455 South 4th Street, Suite 650
Louisville, KY 40202 USA
(502) 574-9033
www.MysteryShop.org

Disney Institute
PO Box 10000
Lake Buena Vista, FL 32830 USA
(321) 939-4600
www.DisneyInstitute.com

Ritz-Carlton Leadership Center
4445 Willard Ave, Suite 800
Chevy Chase, Maryland 20815 USA
(301) 547-4806
www.RitzCarlton.com

Chapter Four

Congratulations, You're a Doctor. Big Deal.

*"If people like you, the will listen to you, but
if they trust you, they will do business with you."*

– ZIG ZIGLAR

Here is the most important thing you need to know about this – you are not entitled to anything. So stop acting like it.

Just graduating dental school and earning the title 'doctor' doesn't put you in a special category of entitlement. This may sound harsh and maybe it deflates you a little bit, but it's the truth. I did the same thing as you. I went to dental school, and beyond, and became a doctor. But earning that title didn't mean that I was entitled to anything. Nothing is handed to you. Not by a long shot.

Forget the idea that you can come to the office, work on teeth, and leave everything else on the back burner while you drive home at 4:30. This is the recipe for an exceptionally-average practice with an average number of patients, average staff productivity, an average revenue, and an average number of patient-to-patient referrals. The most-successful orthodontists realize a dirty little secret that no one in dental school shared with you until now.

Things just aren't that easy.

The most successful people in any field often reach their peak level of status in performance through blood, sweat, and tears. It doesn't matter if they are in real estate, the recording arts, medicine, publishing, professional sports, technology, or even clergy. In a recent exposé on Marissa Mayer, one of the smartest and highest-paid CEO's in Silicon Valley, when asked how she has risen to the helm at Yahoo! at such a young age she responded "I like to work."

No one in a position of power, prestige or high income got where they are simply because of their title or through good genes, luck, or any other excuse that the unsuccessful masses use to relieve themselves of the hard work and results demonstrated and seen by the top one percent in any field. Harsh, but true. It's easier to accept an alibi for your lack of results in life than to risk and fail. Every entrepreneur and top one-percent orthodontists achieved their position through risk, failure, determination, hard work, blood, sweat and tears. Don't think it will be any different for you.

Let's look at a few more famous people who had to take action to get where they are today:

Judd Apatow – Famous for his comedy writing and producing, he tops the lists on being one of the smartest people in Hollywood. Rightfully so. This man didn't just cash in some luck to get where he is. He stayed up late at night to write and re-write scripts by hand while watching Saturday Night Live. Sure, he could have taken the night off, relaxed, and just laughed. But that wasn't enough for him. He wanted to know what it felt like as a young writer to see exceptional comedic writing flow effortlessly from his pen, so he put in the long hours and the

WHAT DO THE FOLLOWING HIGHLY TALENTED PEOPLE HAVE
IN COMMON?

- Woody Allen
- Judd Apatow
- Thomas Edison
- Michael Jordan

Do you have what it takes to be successful?

extreme measures that others in his field avoided by transcribing the words of Saturday Night Live, by hand, over and over again. His hard work and determination helped push him to the top of his industry. Self-sacrifice. Decisive action in pursuit of his goals. He did not wait for an easy button to appear. Reminds me of an old Far Side cartoon with two hungry vultures waiting for their next meal. The caption reads: "screw this, let's go kill something." When will you stop waiting around for everything to go your way without devoting massive effort? It's simply not that easy.

Woody Allen – You are probably familiar with Woody Allen and some of his work. Famous and accomplished actors have been known to blindly accept offers to work with Woody without reading the script or having so much as a clue what the movie is about, where it will be filmed, or even what role they will play. Cate Blanchett describes the phone call for her leading role in *Blue Jasmine*. Without knowing a single detail, other than that she would be working with Woody, she said yes before the voice on the other end of the phone could finish a sentence. But don't believe for a second he became successful because it was all handed to him. No, he had to work hard for it and he did so by putting in a lot of hours of practice. He spent decades practicing his craft in order to become the sought-after director he is. In addition to his film career, Woody Allen is also an accomplished clarinet player who spends three to four hours per day practicing. When asked why he spends so much time at the clarinet, he answers "because I want to be taken seriously and play professionally. I don't want to be asked to play because I'm Woody Allen, I want to be asked to play because I'm good enough to play the clarinet with jazz professionals, and to do that

I have to practice for many hours per day." Hard work — not a single successful person is allergic to it.

Thomas Edison – When you think of Thomas Edison you probably think of a really successful guy who had a lot of skill and intuition. And you would be right. But what you may not realize is that he had many more failures than he had successes. He just didn't focus on those failures. He paid more attention to the successes and kept on going. Failed attempts were either pushed aside or where used as learning experiences so he could go on to something that may be more successful. When asked about his many unsuccessful attempts at developing the lightbulb, he stated "I didn't invent the lightbulb, but instead found 10,000 ways *not* to invent the lightbulb."

Michael Jordan – You know he was good, but that doesn't mean he was born that way. Rather, he put in more effort training and becoming the best of the best than most people could imagine. While there are trainers and specialists that work with the basketball teams, he went above and beyond. Michael went outside the team and hired his own coaches and did his own training regimens. He had dedication to personal improvement when other players simply wouldn't put in the same amount of time. If you asked him to retell the stories of last-second, game-winning shots, he would quickly redirect the conversation to all of the times he had the opportunity to win the game but failed. Imagine that. The greatest basketball player on earth and he quickly focused on his relatively-infinitesimal number of failures. He was always focused on doing better and quick to recognize that doing better meant hard work, not luck, not genes, nor resting on prior successes.

It's easy to say that people are successful because they had it handed to them, or because they were just born with something special. Shrugging off their massive success makes it easier to forget about your own lack thereof. That's because if you really believed that we all have the ability to achieve superstar status you would start asking yourself why you have not yet achieved all you desire and what you are doing wrong.

In other words, you would know it's time to take action and make things happen.

But sometimes it's easier to live with the excuses we've accepted in our heads. Specialists complain about relying on the general dentist, but do nothing to foster those relationships. They complain that their employees won't ask for referrals but do nothing to train, encourage or praise the results when they happen. If it is imperative that you improve referral communication and strengthen referral sources, or cut them loose and become your own number one referral source through positioning, office experience, customer service, and marketing; it also imperative that you decide today, once and for all, to abandon the excuses in your head forever. When we complain about our position with referring doctors or the referral relationship we have with our patients, we are really making a statement about our own engagement and responsibility to our practices. You cannot complain on one hand without criticizing yourself on the other.

The choice is yours. Will you focus on building referral relationships? Will you turn your focus toward positioning yourself without the need to rely on general dentists for your referrals? Or will you strengthen both areas to build a foundation of stability in your practice? If you don't know how many new patients will call your office tomorrow, next week, next month with near-certainty, you are getting this wrong. Unfortunately, none of us were taught how to manage and leverage these essential success strategies in dental school. For the doctors with serious interest, resources are available (including those presented here and in a brief commercial message at the end of this book) to help propel your practice into the position necessary to explode your success over the next ten or twenty years. The solutions I present are not easy but they are tested and proven, not only in our field but throughout the business world in general. You do not need to be exceptionally charismatic to apply them, nor do you have to turn your employees into sleazy used car salesmen to operate in the top one percent of orthodontic practices. You need only to follow simple directions and formulas, take responsibility and get started. Graduating from dental school was truly just the beginning for you.

Chapter Five

Chances Are You Will Retire Poor

"Wealth is the ability to fully experience life."

– HENRY DAVID THOREAU

This one comes as a shock to many and it should. You most likely did not kick and scratch your way through dental school, come out with mountains of debt to prove it, only to retire poor. But that is the reality for most people in the dental field. The percentage is high of all dentists that will make this crucial mistake. Problem is, it is one that could be completely avoided if they just took appropriate action.

How exactly does this happen, you may wonder? After all, you spend an entire career working hard in your practice, making a decent salary, only to walk away in the end with nothing. How can that be? Well, I will tell you how it can be, but you may not like the reality of it, because it largely comes down to you and what you do during your career.

What you do now and in the coming years is going to be the difference between whether or not you retire poor or you get to continue living the lifestyle you deserve. It comes down to you and your decision making.

Most dentists, around 89 percent, will not retire with the same amount of retirement income as they had when they were actively practicing. Shame on us. We can do so much better than that.

Lifestyle choices while in practice are one thing, but it's a completely different ball of wax to allow a gross underestimation of the level of revenue and how to invest, when to buy a building versus lease one, and how to leverage your number one business expenses – payroll – into an army of advocates that can build your retirement at the same time they are building their own through a company-sponsored retirement plan.

When you consider 89 percent of us will retire with less income than we now enjoy, it's as if we act in willful ignorance. It reminds me of a recent commercial for Capital One featuring Alec Baldwin. In the commercial he plays a substitute teacher who asks the classroom what they have been studying with their teacher. The kids say "spelling," to which he replies "that's not a subject, that's an app on your phone." Because spell check apps are available, we're actually *proud* to announce that we no longer have to think for ourselves. We get a free pass to turn off our brains.

Willful ignorance.

Today's doctors are willfully ignorant about the discipline and financial security they know is important but still just out of grasp and as such they are leaving money on the table throughout their careers, and a whole lot of money behind once they finally retire. You have a choice to make about this. You don't have to be willfully ignorant. You can choose right here and now to learn everything you can and put it all into action so that you don't retire poor.

89%

of Doctors Won't Make the
Same Income in Retirement
That They Did While
in Practice

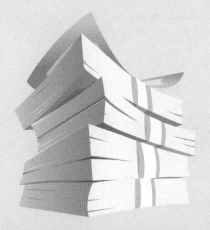

What will your retirement look like?

most-successful individuals in any field, and it won't happen for you. You cannot sail through your career, avoiding the hard decisions and neglecting the path less-traveled, and still achieve wild success and an epic retirement.

You must take full responsibility to run your practice successfully. Not just successfully, but effectively and to *your* advantage. That takes the willingness to leave ignorance behind. It means investing in yourself, your career, and in the information and strategies you need to help you achieve the level of success you dreamed of when you first applied to professional school. That's a commitment I made to myself long ago and it's paid off tremendously.

Are you ready and willing to make that commitment for you, the success of your practice, and so that you can retire maintaining a lifestyle you want? Are you ready to understand what acquisition costs are, how much you spend on each prospect in your marketing and advertising, what type of return on investment each employee is earning for your business and how to leverage every single dollar of income in your business so that your children can go to the kind of school they desire, so that your employees can retire comfortably just like you, so that your community, church or synagogue can benefit from your generosity? Only *you* can answer these questions, learn as much as you can, and put knowledge into action.

Don't let your career rely on an app, like the Capital One commercial I mentioned, thereby choosing ignorance. You spent years going to school, developing the skills to practice your craft. Don't let that be wasted, or short-changed, by willfully ignoring the key puzzle pieces that can let your talents soar. Recognizing this truth — that the top producers in any field are paid more for *who they are* rather than *what they do* is the single-most important realization you must acknowledge before you gleefully take the road less-traveled. It's the difference between having a mediocre practice and one that is highly successful. It is going to be the difference between retiring poor or enjoying an epic retirement.

You hold all the cards to make the difference here. As the saying goes, you can lead a horse to water, but you can't make it drink. I can tell you what you need to learn and how particular things will impact your practice results, but I can't make you take the next steps in learning them. I also can't make you apply those principles once you do make the commitment to learn them.

It all comes down to you, your decisions, and what you want your future, both during your career and in retirement, to look like. Put yourself under intense self-assessment and finally make the decisions that will help get you where you want to be. And if you're not familiar with some of the classic business literature in the magical and mysterious place often unvisited by most doctors after graduation (called the library), I've summarized a few here for your reference. If you read them and apply them, I've also saved you at least one year's tuition in obtaining your M.B.A. You're welcome.

Required Business Reading

Christensen, Clayton. *The Innovator's Dilemma.* New York: Harper

Drucker, Peter. *The Effective Executive.* New York: Harper Collins.

Gerber, Michael. *The E-Myth Revisited.* New York: Harper Collins.

Goleman, Daniel. *Emotional Intelligence.* New York: Bantam.

Levitt, Ted. *Marketing Myopia.* Boston: Harvard Business Press.

Porter, Michael. *Competitive Strategy.* New York: Free Press.

Chapter Six

Your Patients Don't Care About
Your Latest Gadget or C.E. Course

*"Twenty years from now you will be more disappointed by
the things that you didn't do than by the ones you did do."*

– MARK TWAIN

Yes, you may be excited about the latest gadget you purchased. Or maybe about a new continuing education course you attended. But in all honesty that stuff doesn't mean anything to your patients. Disappointed? Well think about when the shoe is on the other foot. Are you excited when you learn about a new gadget that the plumber has when he comes out to fix your toilet? Probably not. Sure, there are a few exceptions to every rule, but most people tend to not care about such things.

There is one thing that people care about when it comes to the latest gadgets you've purchased or courses you've attended. That's how these things will benefit them. Not you, but them. This goes back to the first principle discussed in this handbook. It's not about you. It's about them.

If you can't tell your patients in plain language how the latest and greatest thing is going to benefit them, then don't even mention it. Telling them about it will mean nothing, may irritate them, and the time could be better spent. If it is something that will benefit them, then by all means tell them. But forget the behind-the-curtain info about the device. Instead, boil it down to what it means for them. How will it make their life easier?

More comfortable? Tell them exactly what it will do for them. That is something they will understand, be able to relate to, and will appreciate because they will benefiting in the long run.

I have another news flash for you. The patients that walk into your office, or who are at home looking at your website and wondering if they should make an appointment with you, also don't care about your particular association with any "occlusion camps." If you mention you studied at Pankey or Dawson it means absolutely nothing to them. They have most likely never heard of these places and won't be impressed simply because you take a lot of continuing education. They *assume* you take a lot of continuing education. You are a *doctor* after all. What they really care about, again, is *how this is going to benefit them.*

Let your patients know everything you have done and are doing that will benefit them. If you spent $30,000 and months of your life studying at Pankey or Dawson or any other continuing education that you feel might benefit your patient, by all means talk about it, but in plain language that describes how your advanced training actually benefits the patient. Outside of that conversation, your voice sounds like the parents on the famous Peanuts cartoon classic with Charlie Brown ("mwa, mwa, mwa, mwa") and does nothing to help the patient, or your case conversion rate for that matter. However, getting clear explanations in plain terms about how your training helps make their life easier will make them feel good about making the decision to do business with you over the competition.

Remember, it's not about you. It's about them. And they want to know how everything in your practice will benefit them.

Not only will your patients will not remember your gadgets, they won't remember where you studied or the latest and greatest class you took. There is one thing they will remember though – how you made them feel.

How you make every patient feel is going to stick with them forever. It's a feeling that is going arise every time they think about you and your office. It's going to come into play every time they have a problem with some of the work you did, or if they love their teeth. They will always remember how you made them feel.

Since patients will only remember how you made them feel it is important to give them all top-notch care and treatment. This is crucial if you expect them to continue feeling warm and fuzzy about you ten years from now. I can assure you that nothing says "well, shit" like a crown that has come off nine times. You must do excellent quality dentistry if you plan to be in business ten years from now. But don't stop there. If you provide excellent quality dentistry but you cannot communicate to the patient why they should follow your advice, how they can benefit from the options in your practice, and consistently thank them for their business while making them feel good, you might be in business in ten years, but probably on life support while one of my clients is kicking ass, taking names and eating your lunch.

Treat your patients well, build relationships with them, provide excellent service, and you will create "raving-fan" loyalty. You will also have patients who send you referrals on a regular basis. Whether people are happy with their dentist or not, they love to share their experiences with others. But you want to make sure that it's positive information that they are sharing with their friends and family.

Believe it or not, you do have control over this.

Your control over referrals comes down to how well you treat your patients. Each and every patient, each and every visit. They are all valuable. Together they make up the most important thing in your office, remember?

Focus on excellent service. This needs to come from everyone in your office, not just you. Consider again how important it is to have the right employee in each position in your office and that all employees on board with your mission of providing the best possible patient care. Train your employees with effective and patient-focused scripting so they can communicate everything you are doing that will benefit the patient. If you need help scripting your employees, refer to the resources in Chapter 3 for the Disney Institute and the Ritz-Carlton customer service training.

When you start getting this right, you will elevate your practice to a new level of success. Are you ready to make the commitment to? Great! Turn this information into action and make your patients feel amazing. Send them out the door with an inspired attitude about your practice in order to build your reputation and earn more word-of-mouth referrals. And don't think for a second that you can train your employees once in this area and move onto the next issue. Continuous, never-ending training. It's the hallmark of the most-successful companies in the world. Find me a great company earning ten-times revenue over their nearest competitor and I will show you a company with highly-trained employees on a mission to deliver exceptional service to the customer, without fail.

Team Exercises

Take a few minutes each month to set your calendar for upcoming team trainings. Turn these into a workshop and not a lecture. Ask questions, get input, and discover as a team how you might better serve your patients. I've included a few sample topics you might use at your next team workshop training. Get started on these today.

What three products or services in our office do we provide at an exceptional level of quality but no one even knows we do it? How might we better present these services to our patients so that everyone knows exactly how they can benefit from such a product or service?

_____

_____

_____

What products or services have our patients or referring doctors demanded of us even though we have not actively promoted them in our practice newsletter or on our website? Have we taken the time to survey our other patients to see if these products or services might interest them as well? What are the top three reasons why our patients might ask us to start actively educating everyone in the practice about these products or services?

_____

_____

_____

Chapter Seven

You Should Get Out of the
Dentistry Business Altogether

"Courage is being scared to death, but saddling up anyway."

– JOHN WAYNE

That's right. You went to school all these years to learn how to do what you do and here I am telling you to leave it all behind and go in a completely different field. Am I nuts, or do I have a point? Hear me out for a minute and then you make the call.

If you went into dentistry to just take care of teeth you are not alone. There are many dentists out there that want to fill that role. Chances are that's not you since you are reading this and wanting to do more, grow your business, and reach higher levels of success. But if, by chance, it is what you want, I suggest you give me a call. I'll hire you as one of my associates and you can spend your days clocking in, straightening teeth all day, and then heading home at night to do other things. With this arrangement you can simply go home at the end of the day, leave the entire practice behind, and not have to worry about another thing. You can hope everything takes care of itself and you just continue to get a paycheck twice a month.

Doesn't get any easier than that, does it? But did you really get into the field to do that? I have a sneaking suspicion you didn't. I think you want more than that. In fact, I know you want more than that, because I've been where you are.

Here's the important thing you must understand – the most successful clinicians and small business owners realize they have many, many roles that must be managed. This is in addition to being the main "doer" in their practice. If you want a successful practice you are going to have to wear many hats and take on many roles. You can't just straighten teeth all day, clock out at 4:30 and head home, waiting for your paycheck every two weeks. It doesn't work like that if you want to own a successful practice.

It doesn't work like that for me, or anyone else in successful businesses that earn mid seven or eight figures. And it never will.

Am I saying here that you need to know how to run the reception desk, sweep the floors, and straighten teeth all at the same time? Yes, and no. What I am saying is that you need to be proactive in getting the right people and systems in place in each of these areas. Once you get your head straight about what business you're really in and have the correct systems in place, you can go back to straightening teeth all day, or taking the day off to go to a baseball game, and your office will continue to run as it should.

If you decide today to get into the business of building a system that brings patients *to you* with magnetic attraction, where only the most-qualified prospects show up and are thrilled to pay your fees without resistance, than you shall forever banish the "easy" button. Fortunately, you will also reap rewards and success beyond what you can imagine when you finally get this right and join the top one percent of our profession.

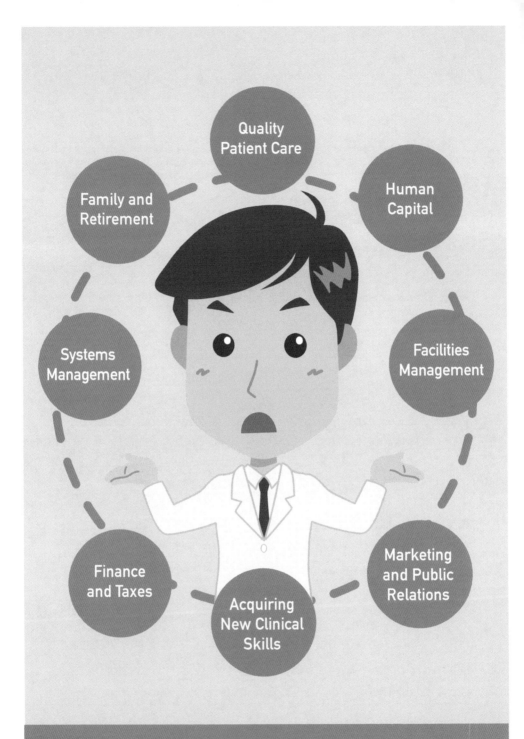

How many hats do you want to wear today?

There is no single solution or easy button to get this done. It takes real commitment to your success and the success of your practice. Discard the idea of easy from your mind all together. A thousand times over you need to resist its temptation. It does not exist for those who wish to create a sophisticated business with true wealth building, legacy building and an epic retirement.

You must have the right systems in place if you want to achieve the level of success you really want. It's just that simple. Are you ready to make the necessary decisions to make that happen? Only you can take the steps to transform your practice.

The bottom line is that it is time to either take action to make it happen, be happy with mediocrity, or just leave the dentistry field all together. The decision is totally up to you.

Looking Toward the Future

There is no way that you learned these seven things in dental school. I didn't learn them either. I have discovered these principles through painful trial and error and from studying some of the great business minds and businesses of our time (e.g., Apple, Disney, Jack Trout, Napoleon Hill, Peter Drucker and Earl Nightingale, to name a few). I have boiled the principles down and implemented the most-successful components in my own practices, so that my business runs exactly the way I want it to. There's nothing wrong with running things on your own terms, as long as you realize what business you are really in. The day I realized that I needed to get out of the dentistry business (i.e., thinking my only job was to work on teeth) and got into the business of building relationships and creating a system that magnetically attracts patients to my practice, I finally saw the massive results I had always dreamed of, without the headaches of more marketing, sleazy sales techniques or turning my staff into "used car salesmen" with high-pressure tactics taught by other practice management consultants. To say my life and my practice changed for the better is the biggest understatement of the century. I finally started to enjoy practice life, I was able to spend more time with my kids, our employees were more satisfied, our patients gave us higher approval ratings and I do it all with one day per week in the clinic.

You can have this, too. I believe in sharing the secrets of success with others. I have taken that to a variety of levels with how I offer seminars, books, and, entire systems that can be put into place for your practice. I want each and every one of you to have the level of success you want to have. I sincerely believe that we have to create the type of world we want by being an active player. I can't sit on the bench, watch my fellow colleagues in the dental field struggle, and just continue on down my road to success and say nothing at all to them. The coach in me won't allow that.

I have to share with you what it is that I know for a fact will make your practice every bit as successful as mine is. By helping you become just as successful, I don't diminish my own success. Go forward and think positive. Put the systems in place to make your practice really take off and reach the next level. One of my favorites, Earl Nightingale, once said "Your problem is to bridge the gap which exists between where you are now and the goal you intend to reach." If you aren't reaching your goals, do not change the goal, change the action steps you are taking towards that goal.

I have provided the tools to help you bridge the gap and navigate your way. Now you have to ask yourself if you will choose to use them.

Made in the USA
Lexington, KY
29 March 2015